Attila P. Kovács
BUDAPEST
FROM SUNRISE TO SUNSET

2015

ATTILA P. KOVÁCS

BUDAPEST
FROM SUNRISE TO SUNSET

Texts by Tibor Berta and Attila P. Kovács

© ATTILA P. KOVÁCS 2015

Published by Pannon-Kultúra Kft.
Photos: Kovács P. Attila • www.kpa.hu
Design, preprint preparation: Kotech Gyorsnyomda
www.quickprint.hu
Print: Pannónia Print Kft.
Translation by Katalin Cseh and Tibor Cseh
Edited and proof read by: Ádám Lázár
Language assistant: Tibor Berta
Second modified edition

ISBN 978-963-89252-8-2

Introduction

As a journalist, in the course of the last decades I interviewed several foreign diplomats, who were temporarily stationed in Budapest for various assignments. During our conversations, almost all of them were quick to emphasize the unique beauty of the city. Oh, come on – one could easily think- they are all diplomats, trained to be polite doing their best to avoid conflicts. They also often voiced that Budapest was a good place to live and praised the city's busy cultural and social life, which would make it particularly hard for them to leave. But eventually, all of them move along. That's what their job is about. Nevertheless, after their official assignments are complete, they often return privately. So could it really be that Budapest is a good place to live in?

And what do we think, we, who spend our entire lives here? Budapest – we live in this city, but do we actually know it? Who else lived here? Who built, destroyed and occupied it? Who passed through, stayed or left it for good? And how many of them? What were its symbols and monuments, and where are they now? When was its golden age – or is it yet to come? When was it, that destruction triggered sudden growth and wealth?

Legend has it, that once Emperor Franz Joseph I. was invited to Buda Castle for the inauguration of St. Stephen's equestrian statue. The artist, Alajos Stróbl approached the Emperor, who was observing his work: 'Your Majesty! How do you like it?' – The Emperor responded: 'I like it, it's a strong horse!'

Another story tells us about Count Gyula Andrássy, who returned to Hungary from a long exile, when the death penalty for his participation in the 1848 Hungarian Revolution was pardoned after the Austro-Hungarian Compromise. Later, Count Andrássy got appointed as the Minister of Foreign Affairs. At his first meeting with Franz Joseph I. the Emperor affectionately greeted him: 'Dear Count, how pleased I am to see you in such a splendid health.' 'Not half as much as I am, Your Majesty!'- he replied.

There are so many legends about the city! Which of them are real and which are fabled? No one knows, but these myths, secrets, unfinished stories are so essentially Budapest! So many wonders and so many secrets yet to de discovered: the buildings, the domes, the ships, the stairs, the sculptures, the colors, the spirits! Have you ever glanced at Budapest from the towers of the Basilica, the St Stephen Cathedral? Did you manage to spot the crow at the Matthias Church? Do you know where the tomb of Gül Baba is?

In his photo album 'Budapest from Sunrise till Sunset', Attila P. Kovács guides us through the well- and less-known sights of the city. He does it from sunrise to sunset, with love, talent, and dedication, for the travelers, for the temporary residents, and even for those of us, who are proud to call Budapest their home. Let's discover the city together, and fall in love with it!

Ádám Lázár

A few words by the author

The story of this book dates back more than eight years, when at my 'Postcards from Budapest' exhibition Géza Varró, my old teacher of photography came up with the idea: 'Why don't you put these photos into an album? It could be entitled "Budapest from Sunrise to Sunset!" His suggestion made me to contemplate over the possibility: well, why not? This book is also a tribute to him. Although he passed away by now his wisdom and legacy will live on forever in our hearts.

First, I started to take thematic photographs of Budapest. By meticulous experiments, I tried to find out how and when the pictures of each sight are to be taken, how to gain the most interesting compositions and the best light conditions. Some of the locations had to be visited more than five or six times. It took me eight years to finish this album. When in September 2012 I completed the photo selection, it occurred to me that many of them were not showing the true picture of Budapest any more – the world, where they were taken, had already faded away. In the last few years, Budapest has transformed so much its image has changed so dramatically that many of the pictures had to be retaken in order to provide the readers with the most up to date views. The Liberty, Elizabeth and Margaret Bridges have been fully reconstructed; the renovation of the St. Stephen Cathedral, the Matthias Church and the Danube side of the Houses of Parliament has been finally completed; the Andrássy Avenue has got a new, red bicycle lane… the list could go on for a while.

In the months after that I walked the streets of Budapest nearly every day, and retook many of the photos. When it came to publishing, I received lots and lots of support from a great number of people. It is impossible to list them all, but I would mention a few, whose help was of key importance to me: Mária Birnbauer, who helped me with the selection of the photos and the layout, Tibor Berta, an excellent tour guide, who kindly contributed by writing the majority of the texts, the GUIDE@HAND, who provided most of the data, and Ádám Lázár, who was both my lector and my editor. We worked tirelessly with Tibor Cseh, the publisher, and Sándor Király from the printing company to publish the book on time, despite the delay caused by retaking of some pictures. I took my last photo only a week before the book was scheduled to be published – it is as fresh as it can get!

Unfortunately, the book is still not entirely complete. I'd like to show you much, much more. Also, several photos and topics had to be left out, but hopefully I will be able to release them in the near future, in another album.

I hope that you, dear reader, will find as much joy and delight in this book, as I enjoyed taking these pictures from my point of view, with great love and dedication, in order to present you the true wonders of the city. I wanted to highlight the different shapes, the colors, the hidden parks, the small statues, the gigantic monuments, and all in all, the everyday beauty of the city I live in. They are there - just turn your head towards them! And don't just look, try to see!

Attila P. Kovács

The first settlement within the borders of Budapest was founded by the Celts on the Buda side. Later the area was occupied by the Romans, who founded the city of Aquincum. In the following centuries the Huns, later the Avars settled here. Hungarian tribes first appeared in the area in the 9th century A.D. King Béla IV. played the major role in the development of Buda as

he built a fortified castle with strong bastions. It was turned into the royal seat during the reign of king Matthías Corvinus, that was the start of its further flourishing. With the merge of three cities, Buda, Pest and Óbuda on November 17, 1873, a new city, Budapest was born. Its name derives from István Széchenyi's book Víĺág dated 1831.

The city is rising

1 700 000 people – 600 000 cars

Turul bird,
the totem animal of the Hungarian mythology

As it is written in the Illuminated Chronicle: "Prince Álmos's mother dreamt of the turul bird, as it flew over her and got her pregnant. And a spring seemed to rise from her womb and many great kings originated from her loins, although they would multiply not in their own lands". The second appearance of the turul bird is connected with the Hungarian Conquest. According to the legend, the migrating Hungarians followed the bird from Levédia, until they lost its sight. That's how they reached Pannonia, the land of Attila. In Buda Castle, on the top of the Habsburg-gate, a huge statue of the turul bird can be seen. The bird seems to be protecting the city with its extended wings. Turul bird is a mythical character of Hungarian legends. It is often depicted as a totem animal. Although the whole Castle was burned to the ground during World War II, the statue of the turul, the guardian of the Habsburg Gate remained intact.

The Castle Hill of Buda

Facing the city of Pest on the opposite bank of the Danube: is The Castle Hill of Buda. The freshwater limestone and tufa, that form the hill's bedrock, are washed by the local streams, thus forming a several kilometers long, multiple-layered cave system. The caves were used as cellars in the Middle Ages, and many of them were also used for military purposes. In the times of the Árpád dynasty, the Castle Hill was used for defensive purposes. Its importance as a fortification became evident after the Mongol invasion, under the reign of King Béla IV. It was chosen instead of the higher Gellért Hill as it had many wells and springs, so in case of the enemy attack, these could provide fresh water. It rose to great importance under the reign of King Matthias Corvinus, when it became the royal seat. In the Ottoman era the bastions were fortified, although their condition deteriorated during the Ottoman occupation. After the Habsburgs' reconquest, everything was renewed. Many buildings, including the Matthias Church were reconstructed in the, dominant baroque style of the time.

Fishermen's Bastion

The Fishermen's Bastion, designed by Frigyes Schulek was built between 1895 and 1902. It is situated between the former Watchtower and the Jesuit Stairs. Its pointed hat shaped stone towers symbolize the seven chieftains of the Hungarians, who led the Conquest of Hungary. The former Bastion of the Fishermen, which existed in the Middle Ages, got its name from the fishermen's guild, which protected that part of the walls of Buda. In that age the guild sold their goods in the market next to Matthias Church. In case of an attack, the members of the guild protected the gates and the bastions heroically. Since 1987 the Fishermen's Bastion has been among the World Heritage Sites.

It is kitsch but it is beautiful. Sir, you can receive the acclamation of the people on the balcony. You can slowly walk on the stairs with the lady. You would have to say that the lady is the Queen and her train is carried by thirty servants. I would suggest that you should give preference to such ladies who like these kinds of things. But keep away from the Stairs of the Jesuits. Once one of my predecessors a jeweller took off to the Castle to sell diamonds to a count and he had not returned ever since. I am convinced that he was murdered on the Stairs of the Jesuits.

Antal Szerb:
Guidebook of Budapest for Martians

Statue of Saint Stephen

The statue of Saint Stephen by Alajos Stróbl is a part of the Fishermen's Bastion. Its neo-romanesque base was designed by Frigyes Schulek, the architect of the Fishermen's Bastion. The statue was completed in 1903, however its inauguration ceremony took place only on May 21, 1906. The base is fringed by oval shaped pierced stone and balustrade railing, which is situated in the center of the southern bastion court. The base is also decorated by the reliefs, portraying the life of Saint Stephen. These reliefs are based on the fresco designs, which were originally to decorate the corridors of the Bastion.

The illuminated Fishermen's Bastion is the highlight of the city

Since the 1980's, reconstructions have grown constant. The Fishermen's Bastion restaurant was completed in 2007. Since 1995 you have to pay an entrance fee to visit the Bastion.

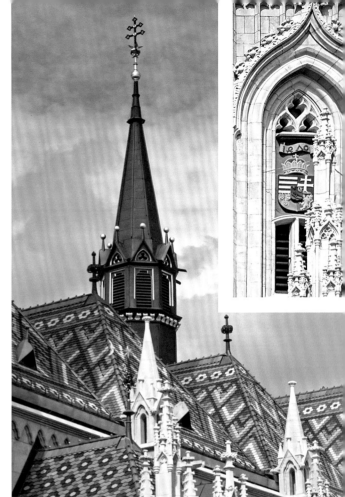

Church of Our Lady, i.e. Matthias Church

A church with many names. Since the population of the Castle District was predominantly German it was first called: German Church. Later they called it: Coronation Church since three kings were crowned her. Most people called it the Church of Our Lady and after some extensive alterations were made by King Matthias they also called it Matthias Church.

Hilton Hotel
and the Matthias Church

After long years of reconstruction, the Church of Matthias is reflected again in its old splendor in the windows of the Hilton Hotel, that opened in 1977. Its towers, decorated with tracery and colorful Zsolnay tiles, greet us from a great distance. Throughout the centuries it has been rebuilt several times. King Béla IV and Matthias Corvinus, were both crowned here. According to the Archdiocese of Esztergom, the first church here was built in 1015 by Saint Stephen, which was most likely demolished by the Mongols. Our "second Founding Father" King Béla IV (1235-1270), erected here a new church, that was first mentioned in 1247. This church was a three-nave cathedral with a transept. Around 1460 Matthias Corvinus erected a royal oratorio next to the southern sanctuary, and also enlarged the right wing tower. On September 2, 1541, the Ottomans tricked the garrison and captured the Castle. They turned the church into a mosque. All the walls were whitewashed, and were covered by carpets. All its decorations were destroyed. One of the chapels, where they stored gunpowder, exploded, and the wall collapsed on the praying then panic stricken and fleeing Turks, to whom the statue of Virgin Mary's appeared. That was the time when the Turks left Buda. Later the church belonged to the Jesuits, who rebuilt it in Baroque style. In the Matthias Church, after the Compromise in 1867, János Simor, Cardinal Archbishop crowned the Austrian Emperor, Franz Joseph I, King and his wife, Elizabeth, Queen of Hungary. In 1873, following the Royal decree, a large scale reconstruction took place, which lasted until 1896. The work was supervised by Frigyes Schulek. After its completion, the church received today's shape. The front hall was built in front of the Maria Gate, and Saint Stephen Chapel was erected on the ruins of the Gari Chapel. The baroque chapels connected to the northern nave were rebuilt in the neo-gothic style.

Buda enjoyed its golden age in the second half of the 15th Century. One of the greatest Christian kings of his time, Matthias Corvinus rebuilt and expanded the palace. His reign brought material and intellectual prosperity upon Buda. The king's Italian courtiers, bureaucrats, soldiers, scientists and artists settled in the city, which resulted in a great spiritual revival. Both, well decorated palaces and public houses were built. The sophisticated and enlightened air of Renaissance permeated the city. In 1541 the city was captured by Suleiman the Great. The steady decline of the Ottoman era ended after it was reconquered by Eugen von Savoy. However, the Habsburgs' victory didn't bring immediate prosperity to Buda. It had to wait until 1873 when Budapest was founded. After that the new royal palace was built, as well as many public houses and offices. The Matthias Church was renovated and the Fishermen's Bastion was also completed. Due to these events the Castle got a new image, which was intact until World War II. During the siege of Budapest the Castle could have been saved from destruction, if the German troops had given it up. But they didn't, in fact, their defense here lasted until the very last day of the siege. The Castle District still bears the traces of the terrible fight. However, most of the houses and buildings, including the Royal Palace have been reconstructed. The latter was finished in the 1970's. Nowadays it is home to one of the most beautiful museums of the country, the National Gallery, as well as to the National Széchényi Library.

Sándor Palace

The building, on the northern side of Saint George Square, had seen a lot since its completion in 1806. During the 1849 War of Independence, only the fierce siege enabled the Hungarian troops to recapture the Royal Palace and Saint George Square. The Sándor Palace was also damaged. After the defeat of the Hungarians, the reconstruction of the Royal Palace took a long time, so the appointed regent of Hungary, was forced to settle in Sándor Palace, which was in a much better condition. Later on, 20 consequent Hungarian prime ministers lived and worked here. Nevertheless, World War II brought destruction to Sándor Palace as well. The little that survived the air raids was taken away by looters. After the war, the building only received a preservative restoration. The crumbling building hosted interesting exhibitions for many years. The decision on the full scale reconstruction was made in 1997, which was followed by a profound archaeological research. The reconstruction was completed in 2002. The interior gained back the atmosphere of the early 19th century. Some rooms and furniture were partially restored according to archive photos, others were replaced with objects of similar age. Today the old splendor of Sándor Palace's shines again, and it's also the residence of the President of Hungary.

The Great Rondella of Buda Castle is a round bastion situated on the southern slopes of the Castle Hill. It's a part of the reconstructed old defense system of Buda Castle. Accompanied by the excavation, conservation and supplement of its walls from the Middle Ages, its full restoration was completed in the 1950s. Its impressive five-meter-thick walls were equipped with seven cannon portholes and were built on the steep outside slopes. The Great Rondella with the Mace Tower is one of the most characteristic buildings in the southern part of the Castle.

Buda Castle Funicular

The construction of the originally steam powered funicular was István Széchenyi's son's, Ödön Széchenyi's initiative. In 1870, the second funicular in Europe was inaugurated in Buda. It was seriously damaged during World War II, and looted in 1948-49. The long awaited reopening of the funicular took place after the complete reconstruction on June 6, 1986. It transports more than 500.000 visitors a year. In 2012 a one-way ticket costs 900 forints.

Buda Castle Tunnel

The construction of the tunnel, designed by Adam Clark, started in 1853. The tunneling of the 350-meter-long tunnel took seven and a half months. It was finally completed in 1857. Until 1918 everybody had to pay a fee to go through. In 1973 it was renewed, and equipped with a new ventilation system to celebrate the centenary anniversary of the merge of Buda, Pest and Óbuda, One of the entrances to the 7000 m2 nuclear-proof Castle Bunker opens from the Tunnel.

Zero Kilometer Stone

In a small park, facing the Funicular, you can come across the Zero Kilometer Stone. This is the starting point to measure the length of the Hungarian motorways and main roads. The original statue of the guardian angel of the travelers was relocated from the Castle to the south-western part of this park after the construction of the Chain Bridge began. However, the angel was reported missing in 1932. Thus on the Hungarian Automobile Club's initiative, a Madonna statue resembling a milestone was erected on the exact spot of the 0 kilometer. The monument was destroyed during World War II, so in 1953 it was replaced with a limestone statue of a worker who is gazing in the distance. A motive that was so typical at the time of social realism. As a sign of weakening of the system, in 1974 the worker's statue was replaced by Miklós Borsos' work, a 3-meter-tall limestone statue of a stylized 0.

Hungarian Coat of Arms

On the wall you can see a big coat of arms with the present coat of arms in the middle as it was adopted in 1990. Some of its elements date back to the 13th Century, such as the sharp, split shield, that is divided into seven, red and silver Árpád stripes. The double cross originates from Byzantium, and it is the symbol of the Christian monarchy. The three hills, supporting the cross, date back to the 15th century. It was also the time when the Hungarian Holy Crown appeared at the top of the coat of arms. A still valid, 16th century interpretation says that the double cross symbolizes the Apostolic Kingdom, the three hills symbolize three mountains, the Mátra, the Fátra and the Tátra, while the four silver stripes symbolize the four most important rivers: the Danube, the Tisza, the Dráva and the Száva. The coat of arms in this form became the symbol of the whole country in the 16th Century. However, in 1849, after the Habsburg dynasty was dethroned, the crown disappeared from it and the curved shield shaped Kossuth's coat of arms came into force.

New modifications followed the Austro-Hungarian Compromise in 1867. At that time the old coat of arms became the central one, surrounded by the coats of arms of the partnering countries: Croatia, Transylvania, Slavonia, Dalmatia and Fiume. This is what can be seen today on the wall next to the funicular. Except short periods, when it was briefly replaced by the simpler Kossuth's coat of arms, this coat of arms was used until the communist dictatorship started in 1949. After the 1989 regime change, we turned back to the original, oldest motive and since then we have been proudly using our coat of arms as a national symbol.

Hungarian Parliament Building

The Parliament was built in an eclectic style, with neo-gothic as a leading style. Europe's second largest Parliament building dominates the Pest bank of the Danube with its graceful, scalloped carved towers. The Parliament has become one of the symbols of the Hungarian capital. On Kossuth Square one can find two other buildings designed for the same competition. The winner of the contest became the Parliament building one of the other entries ended up as one of the most important ministries: The Ministry of Agriculture and the other ended up as a museum. For many decades on the top of the Parliament building a huge illuminated red star was shining indicating who were the rulers of the country between 1947- 1989. For almost the entire life of the building a constant restoration work with scaffoldings on one side or the other signalled that the soft stones of the building had to be changed one by one. Now outside the Parliament a huge Hungarian flag and a memorial of the heroes of the Hungarian Uprising of 1956 were erected. Some people felt that it was of some significance that prior to the construction work begun the place had to be filled up considerably and the material used was rubbish.

50

The Houses of Parliament was designed by Imre Steindl. Though it is baroque in side in style and mass effect, the building is basically neo-gothic in details. Exclusive use of local Hungarian materials was a key criterion for the tender. The only exception is the eight, six-meter high marble monolith columns at the main stairs, which were brought from Sweden. The construction lasted until 1904, which didn't let the designer see its completion. The construction began on Tömő Square on October 12, 1885. During the seventeen years of construction, an average number of 1000 people worked there, having moved 176 000 cubic meters of ground and used 40 million bricks, and 40 kg of gold. The building itself is 268 meters long, 123 meters wide, its area is 17 745 m² and its volume is 473 000 cubic meters. It is not by chance that its highest point is 96 meters. The original plan was to finish it for the Hungarian Millennium in 1896. That's why it was designed to be exactly 96 meters high. Beside the Parliament, only Saint Stephen Cathedral is so high, that makes them both the second tallest buildings of the country, only 4 meters behind the Esztergom Cathedral. They are higher than any other building in Hungary, including television towers. Its central element is the dome, which is flanked by the House of Representatives (today's Parliament), and the House of Lords (today's Congress Hall). The building has 27 gates, 29 staircases and 13 passenger and freight elevators inside. It also gives home to more than 200 offices. Inside and outside there are altogether 242 sculptures on the walls (90 outdoors and 152 indoors). Prominent frescoes and paintings also decorate the Parliament. The 22-23 carat gold used for the decoration makes up 40 kg altogether. Its Danube side's reconstruction finished after 21 years of work in September 2009. The public could first enjoy the illumination of that side on August 20th, 2011.

The dome of the Parliament rises above the Holy Crown

Since 2000, the Hungarian Holy Crown has been placed in the hall under the dome. It is guarded by the crown guards, who resumed their work after 66-year break in 2011. The crown is called holy, because it came from Rome, with the blessing of the Pope, and it symbolized the reconciliation between the Hungarians and Christian Europe. According to researches the crown was made in a Georgian foundry. In addition, the Holy Crown symbolizes the spirit of the Regnum Marianum, that originates dates back to 1038, when the founder of the Kingdom of Hungary Saint Stephen on his dying bed, offered his crown and country to Virgin Mary. The crown is particularly unique, because according to the ancient Hungarian legal system, the supreme power belonged to the crown and not to the king who was wearing it.

Holy Crown

The crown symbolizes both the land and the people of the country, or as the Pope said in 1198: "The honor of the country originates and is rooted in the crown". The path to legitimate power has always led through the crown, and even then could never be absolute, since only the crown's power was absolute. The crown is an independent legal entity, which is separated from the king. The free Hungarians obedience and loyalty always belonged to the crown, not to the king. That's why not every rebellion against the king was treason. Sometimes it was their legal right and duty. However, any action against the Holy Crown, the unity and the interests of the nation was treason. Due to the holiness of the crown, the coronation ceremony had its own scenario. It always took place in the Coronation Church of Székesfehérvár, and only the Archbishop of Esztergom could place the crown on the head of the king. In the absence of these two conditions, the monarch could not have the legitimate power of the crown.

Hungarian Academy of Sciences

At the Pozsony session of the Parliament, on November 3rd, 1825, Count István Széchenyi donated part of his properties' annual income, which made up for 60 000 forints, to establish the Hungarian Scholar Society. His generous offer encouraged other noblemen to donate significant amounts for this purpose. The construction started in 1862, under Miklós Ybl and Antal Szkalnitzky's supervision. The frescoes in the ceremonial hall were painted by Károly Lotz. The building was completed in 1865.

Pest Vigadó

The building was designed by Frigyes Feszl in 1858 and its construction was completed in 1865. The interior is decorated with the ballad-themed frescoes by Károly Lotz and Mór Than. Franz Liszt visited Pest to participate in the opening ceremony, where he performed his oratorio, the Legend of Saint Elizabeth. The Vigadó was heavily damaged during World War II. The reconstruction started in the 1970s and was completed in 1980. However, in 2004 the renovation started again.

Saint Stephen Basilica

The Basilica is the tallest building of the city centre. Its dome is 96 meters high, that equals the height of the Parliament. These two buildings symbolize the ecclesiastic and secular power. Both of them are equally high and equally outstanding. The number 96 refers to the year of planned completion of the church; it was to be finished by 1896 to celebrate the Millennium of the Hungarian Conquest. Interestingly the name basilica doesn't refer to its size, nor to its architectural characteristics, but its religious rank. In 1931, the Pope's representative granted the "Basilica minor", or small basilica rank to the church to commemorate Prince Saint Imre's death's 900th anniversary. Outside the dome, a look-out has been constructed with a spectacular view over the city. In addition we can learn here about Hungary's largest the Saint Stephen Bell. The look-out can easily be reached with the elevator, but the enthusiasts can take the traditional way and climb 364 stairs. According to the original plans of its first

designer, József Hild, the cathedral would have been a more narrow and compact building. The western main façade would have been framed by corinthian column portico with 4 huge pillars at its sides. The Basilica gained today's form thanks to the new designer, Miklós Ybl's revision to the original plan. The facade has undergone the most significant changes.

Hungary's largest bell, is placed in the southern (right) tower, was created in the Perner foundry in Passau, in 1990. It weighs 9250 kg with the bottom diameter of 240 cm. The interior decorative painting and gilding work was mainly carried out by Robert Scholtz. In 1971 the storage space for the Holy Right was constructed behind the sanctuary, in a chapel. The Holy Right means the right hand of king Saint Stephen which was cut off and conserved after death of the great king. Since 1971 the Saint Stephen Cathedral is the final guarding place of the Holy Right. The most important part of the relic's cult is the annual Holy Right procession on 20th August.

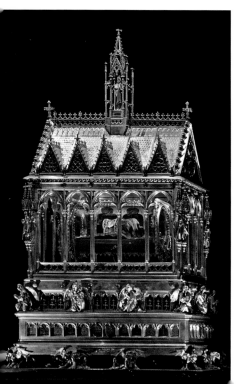

From the top of the Cathedral you can enjoy a spectacular view. The whole city lies below your feet. The impressive size of the dome amazes the visitor; it shows a completely different face of the dome from up there. Its designer József Hild made a significant static error. As a result, after 22 years of building work, the dome collapsed with a great bang in 1868.

Hungarian National Opera House

In the 1870s, the National Theatre, that hosted both opera and drama performances, could no longer satisfy demands. A new, separate Opera house was badly needed. Most of the expenses were covered by the Court's art budget. However, Franz Joseph I. stipulated that the Opera House must not surpass the Vienna Opera House. Although the designer, Miklós Ybl's hands were tied from the beginning, he managed to design a beautiful, imposing building, that was also very modern for its age. It had a hydraulically operated lifting and circular stage, and instead of traditional backstage scenes movable stage elements were operated from the top. A rain machine and an iron curtain were responsible for the fire protection. The construction began in 1875. And instead of the planned 5 years, it took 9 years to finish it, due to the budget miscalculations and slowly arriving revenues. In addition to his architectural duties, Miklós Ybl himself designed all small details such as the handle bars and lamps as well.

The interior of the Opera House is even more spectacular than its exterior, it is even said to rival the Paris Opera. All details, consoles and carvings praise the fantasy and the sense of beauty of their designer Miklós Ybl. The ceiling above the 1100-seat auditorium is decorated by Károly Lotz's frescoes. After its inauguration, the royal couple Franz Joseph I and Queen Elizabeth were regular guests here. The royal box could only be used by the Queen in the King's presence, so when she came alone, she had to choose another box. It was only typical of her vanity to reserve the first box on the left, next to the main stage, so that she could always be in the spotlight, even if the box could not provide the best opera experience.

Chain Bridge

The first permanent bridge of the capital became the symbol of the city and the country. The bridge replaced the former extended chain of the customs office, which span across the Danube and ended in a customs house on each side. The construction was commissioned by Count István Széchenyi. The bridge connects Adam Clark Square on the Buda side to adjacent István Széchenyi Square on the Pest side. The name originates from its linked chain supporting structure, stretched between the two, triumph arch-like pillars. The iron pieces are held together by hundreds of thousands of rivets. At summer weekends the bridge is closed to car traffic, thus transforming into a pedestrian bridge, where numerous programs and attractions entertain the passers by. Even if we stop to take a look at the spectacular view of Buda and Pest, it doesn't take more than a couple of minutes to cross the bridge. Yet, the prominent author of the early 20th century, Antal Szerb, writes in such a praising way about the bridge in his Budapest Guide: "Take a walk with a lady to Buda, and then come back, possibly with the same woman. You'll see she'll confess you love, because the bridge is so long". The preparations for the construction and solutions to the emerging technical and financial problems are all due to the hard work of Count István Széchenyi. It was him who initiated the construction, and Baron György Sina who financed it. The Chain Bridge was the first permanent bridge between Buda and Pest and on the whole Danube's length in Hungary as well. The bridge was opened for the traffic on November 20th, 1849. However, on the Buda bridgehead the date of November 21 is written, which marks the beginning of the toll collection. The only person who could never cross the bridge was the one who created it. Count István Széchenyi's death prevented him from ever doing it.

Liberty Bridge

The Liberty Bridge is the shortest of all Budapest bridges. It proved to be the most resilient bridge during the siege of Budapest in World War II – the German forces were unable to fully destroy it. It was reopened on August 20th, 1946. Later, in 1980, it underwent a massive reconstruction, when its entire inner structure was replaced by steel elements. It was then that the bridge regained its trademark green colour – after the war it was painted a greyish blue colour as it was the only available type of paint at the time.

Margaret Bridge

Margaret Bridge, the second oldest bridge of Budapest, was inaugurated on April 30th, 1876, five years after the construction plan was announced. It has the unique structure as it is divided into two by Margaret Island thus adjusting to the two different down streams of the Danube. The exit to Margaret Island was only finished in 1900, with only the boat access available before. In 1935-37, the bridge was extended to its current four-laned form, with a tramway passing in between. On November 4th, 1944, its Pest wing exploded during the afternoon rush hour. The explosion

was not planned to happen that time, but accidentally a tram pantograph touched the railway wiring, triggering the activation of the explosive fuse, that was passing underneath, resulting in a tragically high death toll. On January 18th, 1945, the Buda end also suffered an attack. After the war, it was fully reconstructed by 1948. The bridge underwent major renovations in 1978 and in 2009. During the latter, it was out of service for almost two years, reopening in June 2011. The original plan was to restore its pre-World War appearance as much as possible: wrought iron lamps and light suspensions were erected, the iron-concrete slabs were replaced by more durable steel elements, and the handrails were entirely reconstructed. The arc of the middle curve was cut down, the road was widened, and a bicycle lane was constructed, adding two extra meters to its width. The job of the constructors was acknowledged by the 2012 European Steel Bridges Award.

Elizabeth Bridge

Inaugurated in 1903, it was the longest spanning chain bridge of the world for 23 years. Overlooking the bridge from the hill on the Buda side is the statue of the missionary priest sent by the Pope to strengthen christianity in Hungary. According to some legends the Italian priest: Gerald (Gellért) was not a flexible diplomat and following an argument some of his Hungarian opponents put him in a nail studded barrel and pushed the barrel off the rocks. As a memory of the event and his influence the hill now carries his name: Gellert Hill. It was reconstructed in 1960-64. The bridge commemorates Queen Elizabeth, wife of the Austrian Emperor Franz Joseph. The Austrian called the Queen Sissi. The Hungarian felt that she was the Habsburg who has done the most for them. Some people felt that the church on the Pest side facing the bridge should be removed so that a direct, straight line of traffic and view could connect the middle of the town and Gellert Hill. Finally a compromise was made the church stayed and the road went around it. In 2011 its impressive illumination was installed, as a courtesy of the Japanese state.

Statue of Queen Elizabeth at Döbrentei Square

Queen Elizabeth of Austria — also known under her affectionate nickname, Sissi — was assassinated on September 10th, 1898, during her vacation at Lake Geneva. The assassin stabbed her in the chest with a sharpened file, that pierced through the left ventricle of her heart. She was buried in the Capuchin Crypt in Vienna, the ancient crypt of the Habsburg dynasty. The entire Hungarian nation mourned the loss of their guardian angel, the Queen of the nation. Amidst the torments of the 19th century, she was the only person in the Habsburg dynasty who was friendly to Hungarians. She endorsed the Austro-Hungarian Compromise in 1867, and continuously represented the Hungarian rights on every possible occasion. She spoke fluent Hungarian: she learnt the first sentences from her first son's, Rudolph's nanny, and later she kept on practising with Ida Ferenczy, a Hungarian royal duenna. She even took lessons from famous, Budapest-based journalist, Miksa Falk. Her first child, Marie Valerie, was considered to be a Hungarian baby, as she was born in Buda, and raised in a Hungarian way, according to the special request of her mother. She also preferred Hungarians as maids of honour. Her favourite hangout was Grassakovich Castle in Gödöllő, that was one of the country's gifts to the royal couple after their coronation. She practically achieved a celebrity status in the 20th century, and she is still one of the most popular historical figures in Hungary. Numerous public spaces, buildings and institutes bear her name, and she also inspired countless books, plays, and movies. Her statue was erected in Döbrentei Square, by the Buda end of the bridge that was named after her.

Elizabeth Lookout on János Hill

János Hill had been a popular local hangout way before the lookout was constructed. Its name originates from an old Hungarian myth, that tells the story of the famous soldier, János Hunyadi, whose life was saved on this spot by María, a young Greek beauty. The hill is the highest point of Budapest, offering the best views of the city from its 528 metre height. Close to its top, a small tunnel was formed inside the dolomite structures. Originally, the hill was named Pozsonyi Hill, as in the 19th century it was possible to see as far as Pozsony (Bratislava) from its highest point. But just like with all its other formalized successors (Marta Cliff, Elizabeth Peak), it wasn't able to replace the popular old name, so after a while, János Hill was accepted as an official title, and Pozsonyi Hill was preserved as the name of a smaller, north-eastern slope. As the highest point of the capital, János Hill was a popular spot for meteorological observations, and even a laboratory was installed in the lookout after its erection in 1910. According to scientists, air here is drier, colder, and less humid than in the metropolitan area, and the frequent winds help to preserve its excellent quality. The temperature is always warm and sunny, even when the city is covered with heavy fog. The hill was one of the favourite hiking spots of Queen Elizabeth, who made three trips up here in 1882. Her visit was commemorated by the erection of a rock-shaped memorial, and later, in 1910, the main lookout was also named after her. The lookout regained its old charm and beauty after its renovation in 2005.

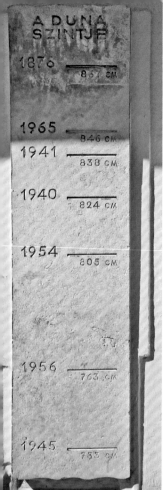

A DUNA
SZINTJE

1876 ———— 867 CM

1965 ———— 846 CM
1941 ———— 838 CM

1940 ———— 824 CM

1954 ———— 805 CM

1956 ———— 763 CM

1945 ———— 753 CM

Danube peaks at 760 cm

HAJÓÁLLOMÁS · INFORMÁCIÓ · TICKET

June 28, 2009

Trams on the Grand Boulevard

Contrary to the popular belief, the first Budapest tram line wasn't a result of the electrification of an older, horse-powered one. It was a brand new construction, built from scratch by the Siemens&Halske company. The new line, that ran between the Nyugati railway station and Király Street, was fully completed in less than sixty days, and was inaugurated on November 28th, 1887. The new generation of Budapest trams, the so called G series, appeared on the streets of the capital just after the Millennium, as a part of the city's policy to unify the appearance of the public transport vehicles. In 1906, 30 of these vehicles were produced. Later, the trams were manufactured by the Hungarian Ganz company, German DÜWAG, and Czechoslovakian Tatra, with brand new Siemens Combino to follow.

Citadel and the Statue of Liberty

The Citadel, this 220-meter long fortress, with 12-16-meter high walls, was constructed by Haynau, the loathed Austrian general. He is hardly the most popular figure in Hungarian history as he coordinated the cruel reprisals after the fall of the 1848-49 Hungarian Uprising. Unlike other similar fortresses, the Citadel served not for the protection of the city, but rather for the intimidation of the citizens of Budapest – most of its cannons were aimed towards the city! The sculptures, constructed by Zsigmond Kisfaludy Strobl, were inaugurated in 1947, and they form a part of the Liberation Memorial. The statue of the Soviet soldier was transferred to the Statue Park after the transition in 1989. The three other pieces were preserved, including the two smaller statues that fight against the dragon symbolizing fascism. The main figure that was erected in the honour of the glorious victory of the Soviet Army, is now a symbol of the freedom and independence of the Hungarian nation. The monumental Statue of Liberty is towering over the city with its 40 meter height; in its head there is enough space for four adults!

Synagogue of Dohány Street

This monumental, neo-Moorish building is the largest functioning Synagogue in Europe and the second largest in the world (after the Synagogue of New York). It is widely renowned as one of the most beautiful Synagogues. In his work on its interior design, the architect, Lajos Förchter closely followed the biblical details of the Temple of Solomon, carefully enriching them with elements of Mesopotamian and Islam architecture. He combined these ancient decorative motives with the most modern techniques of his time such as the cast iron structures and the ceiling lights. The two towers represent the strong assimilation tendencies of the Jewish population, as the towers are more common in christian architecture. The outside walls are bricked, with ornamental decorations reminiscenting the relics of the ancient eastern culture. The Grand Synagogue opened its gates in 1859, and it can house up to 3000 visitors. Originally, the Synagogue was open for all Jewish communities, but after the 1868-69 Hungarian Jewish Congress, it became one of the main centres of Neolog Judaism in Hungary.

Tomb of Gül Baba

This tomb is the last remaining Turkish memorial in Eastern Europe that has preserved its original function. The 150 years presence of the Ottoman Empire in Hungary left many memories. The Turks left their influences stayed. They remained in names, in customs in tastes and to some words even in the language. Gül Baba, a Turkish military ruler was named after the rose he used to decorate his hat with. His traditional Turkish style poems survived. The love of flowers by the Turks is also indicated that one of the most expensive parts of Buda is called: The Hill of Roses.

Great Market Hall

The Great Market Hall of Budapest, on Fővám Square, is a unique location to spot traditional, Hungarian specialties. It is a real must!

Budapest food supply was desperately in need of some serious modernization after the city's quick expansion in the 19th century. Based on Paris models, the City Hall commissioned the construction of six steel-structured market halls. The most impressive of these is undoubtedly the Great Market Hall on Fővám Square. It was designed by a lecturer of the University of Technology, Samu Pecz, and the construction works started in 1894. According to the original plans, the inauguration was scheduled for 1896, for the Millennium anniversary of the Hungarian state. Obviously, nothing went as planned: just ten days before the ceremony a fire burnt down the entire roof, so the ceremony had to be postponed for a year until February 15th, 1897. The building quickly gained regional fame, and was even visited by Emperor Franz Joseph I in May of that year. As the majority of the goods were transported to the capital by water, the market hall is connected to the Danube by a small tunnel, and its basement housed the cold storage rooms as well. During the World War I, it was hell here: the prices skyrocketed, and petty theft and fighting was common. It was severely damaged during World War II. It was renovated afterwards, but in 1991 it was declared to be in a life-threatening condition. After serious renovations in 1994 it got restored to its original beauty.

The National Cemetery is one of the most important burial grounds of the country. Here it is easy to knock into memorials of the greatest Hungarians of all times, be it writers like Mihály Vörösmarthy, Károly Kisfaludy, Mihály Táncsics, or János Arany, or politicians, such as Lajos Batthyány or Ferenc Deák.

National Graveyard
Kerepesi Cemetery

At the beginning of the 1840s, the municipality of Budapest realized that they were about to face a cemetery crisis, as the city's main burial grounds were quickly running out of space. In 1847, the magistrate allotted an area to house the new graveyard within the city's actual borders. The citizens were not pleased at all first, as the area was hardly accessible, and the roads there were extremely bad.

Since the 1850s the graveyard's popularity started to increase, as more and more wealthy citizens chose it for their family tomb. The poet Mihály Vörösmarthy was the first famous Hungarian buried here in 1855. Later, the remnants from the Váci Street cemetery, and the most impressive tombs from the Józsefváros graveyard were transferred here, and in 1870, the memorial to the heroes of the 1848 revolution was erected. One of the most famous reburials was that of the influential Hungarian poet, Károly Kisfaludy. Since the 1860s the National Graveyard became the main burial ground of the Hungarian elite, including leading politicians, actors, artists, and businessmen. From that time on, the most famous Hungarian sculptors were entitled to create masterpiece artworks on their tombs. Italian obelisks and tombstones create a truly impressive atmosphere all around the cemetery which was named as the National Pantheon after the burial of Batthyány, a martyr prime minister of the Hungarian revolution of 1848.

Kossuth
Mausoleum

Tombstone of
the
Petőfi family

Famous Hungarians resting here

Endre Ady, János Arany, Lajos Batthyány, Lujza Blaha, Adam Clark, Tivadar Csontváry Kosztka, Ferenc Deák, Loránd Eötvös, Ferenc Erkel, Mór Jókai, Attila József, Frigyes Karinthy, Dezső Kosztolányi, Gyula Krúdy, Ödön Lechner, Károly Lotz, Kálmán Mikszáth, Zsigmond Móricz, Mihály Munkácsy, Miklós Radnóti, Ignác Semmelweis, Mihály Táncsics, Mihály Vörösmarty, Miklós Ybl, and many others.

115

Széchenyi Lookout

Széchenyi Hill used to be a popular hiking spot even in the times of the Austro-Hungarian Compromise, as it provided an excellent view over the metropolitan area and the Danube. It was named after István Széchenyi in 1860, the year of the count's death.

The lookout was constructed according to the plans of Miklós Ybl, and it was first erected on Heroes' Square, on the spot of the present Millennium Monument. The building, towering over an artesian fountain, was doomed to be destroyed after the installation of the Monument, but in 1897, the Svábhegy Association managed to transfer it to its current location on Széchenyi Hill.

The octagonal building, originally named Gloriette, is located at the end of Rege Street. Two rows of staircases lead up here, bordered by stone railings on each side. Cylindrical stone pillars stand at the base of these railings, supporting the arms of Budapest, and the head of a lion. Close to it, we can find the bust statue of István Széchenyi. Its original version was inaugurated in 1891, at the 100th anniversary of his birth. The statue had its fair share of adventures: in 1900, it was stolen for the first time, but one year later it was found in a private collection in Vienna. They reinstalled it to its original location, but in 1997, it was stolen again – presumably not because of its artistic value, but because of its valuable bronze. The statue that we can see now was erected in 2003. So the oldest memorial at the lookout is Széchenyi memorial plate, which dates to 1860.

The Operetta Theatre and the Moulin Rouge

The Somossy Orpheum (now: Operetta Theatre) was built in 1898, in the heyday of the Hungarian art nouveau. The introduction of electric lightning added to its charm as it was a real rarity at that time. Its 116-candle chandelier still hangs over the stage. The Operetta Theatre has successfully preserved the best traditions of the century old Hungarian operetta, and also managed to become the most popular musical theatre of the bustling Budapest scene. In 1923, a luxurious club opened on the ground floor of the building, which was named Moulin Rouge after its Paris counterpart.

Mai Manó House

Opposite the Operetta Theatre, next to the Thalia Theatre you can see a small, art nouveau building, that boasts such an unusual history that it served as an inspiration for several movies and pieces of literature. This eight-storey house was originally constructed as a studio by Manó Mai, an imperial royal photographer and writer. Since 1932, it hosted famous Arizona, a world wide known variety theatre that impressed its audience not only with the high quality performances, but also with its outstanding stagecraft. The modern equipment enabled the staff to lift and rotate the stage, and give the impression of the artists descending from the sky, or of the dancers entering the private boxes hanging down from the fortune worth chandeliers. The heart and soul of the business were Sándor Rozsnyai, the dedicated owner, and Imre Szivós, an excellent engineer. Arizona also employed Rodolfo, the great magician, who sometimes greeted the guests in the cloakroom, carefully picked the pockets of their coats, and later surprised everybody by miraculously presenting their private articles on stage.

Nagymező Street: nightlife's epicentre

It is pretty hard to imagine that 200 years ago this area was covered with cabbage plantations. The reminder of that time is the name of the street: 'big meadow street'. Nowadays, this district houses the city's most impressive theatres and varieties, and it is also easy to find high-class restaurants, busy cocktail bars or lively nightclubs around here. Locals call it: Pest Broadway.

National Theatre

The first one to dream about the Hungarian National Theatre on the banks of the Danube was István Széchenyi himself, who is often called 'the greatest Hungarian'. After long debates on the topic, in 1836 the Parliament finally agreed on the construction of the National Theatre. The institution was first named Hungarian Theatre of Pest, and only in 1840 was renamed into National Theatre. Until 1913, the theatre was housed in the building on the corner of Múzeum Boulevard. And after it was demolished it began its long and adventurous journey all around the city. First, it was transferred to Blaha Lujza Square, to the building of the People's Theatre, which in its turn also had to be demolished in 1965 because of the new metro line construction. As a result, the theatre moved to Nagymező Street, to the location of nowadays' Thália Theatre, and one year later, to Hevesi Sándor Square, to the Hungarian Theatre. After several unsuccessful attempts, the construction of the new National Theatre building started on September 14th, 2000 and lasted for 15 months. The theatre was inaugurated on September 14th, 2002, with Imre Madách's play, The Human Tragedy. Functionally, the building can be divided into three different parts. Its principal centre is a circularly shaped auditorium and a studio stage, surrounded by offices, the technical and commercial areas, and further outside, as the third layer, the whole building is wrapped up in a picturesque, green park. The park houses the life sized statues of several giants of Hungarian theatre history. The theatre itself, situated at the bank of the Danube, gives the impression of a floating ship. Inside, three different stages can house performances simultaneously.

Palace of Arts

Situated on the Danube bank, just next to the National Theatre, the Palace of Arts puts on its fancy party clothes every single night. The playful, constantly changing colours of its night time illumination easily draw everybody's attention to this excellent piece of modern architecture.

Heroes' Square

Towering at the end of the fabulous Andrássy Road, this powerful composition is one of the true jewels of the city. In the elongated axis of the boulevard stands a 36-meter-high corinthian column. It serves as a pedestal for Archangel Gabriel, guardian of Hungary, who holds the Holy Crown, the symbol of the Hungarian state in his right hand, and the double cross, representing the apostolic kingdom, in his left hand. This 5-meter-high statue was created by György Zala, who was gained the Grand Prix of the Universal Exposition of Paris in 1900. The statue of Gabriel is surrounded by the seven chieftains, who founded the Hungarian state in the Carpathian Basin in 895. At the forefront, the Memorial to Hungarian Heroes is displayed, and the whole square is encircled by a monumental column composition and the statues of greates Hungarian kings and governors. It was named Heroes' Square in 1932. Two palaces of Hungarian art, the Art Gallery and the Museum of Fine Arts frame the square on the right and left.

Museum of Fine Arts

The Art Gallery and the Museum of Fine Arts frame the square on the right and left. Both of the buildings were designed by the square's chief architects Albert Schickedanz and Fülöp Herzog. The Museum of Fine Arts boasts a picture collection of 2600 pieces that makes it the world's seventh biggest picture gallery. It also houses a worldwide known El Greco and venetian collection. The museum is also significant from an architecture point of view, and it often receives foreign groups of architects who study the building's interior and exterior structures. The Museum gained a bit of a worldwide attention in 1983, when unknown criminals managed to enter the building and committed a robbery that deprived the collection of 1 billion 436 million HUF (6.7 million USD) worth items. Back then, some headlines called the robbery to be the 'Crime of the Century'. Among the stolen pieces were Raffaello's Esterhazy Madonna, The Portrait of a Young Man, and Tiepolo's Madonna and Saints, and the Rest on the Flight to Egypt. The Hollywood like theft attracted a lot of media attention, and kick-started a powerful investigation, and finally, in January 20, 1984, the pictures were found in a Greek monastery, wrapped up in an old suitcase. Three days later, they were successfully reinstalled, and the museum significantly tightened up its security policy. This was quite a bit of a challange as the premises are often used by foreign embassies to host receptions to commemorate their national days' celebrations. To popularize art the museum also organises birthday parties for children and have party games dealing with knowledge of the exhibits. In the centenary year of 2006, the museum was entirely renovated, and its newly installed illumination adds to its beauty.

Vajdahunyad Castle

The history of Vajdahunyad Castle, currently functioning as the Museum of Agriculture, dates back to the Hungarian Millennium. In the 1890's, Hungary was enthusiastically preparing for the 1000-year anniversary celebration of the Hungarian conquest in 895. At the beginning of the decade, some politicians campaigned for hosting the World Expo – just like the French did for the centenary of the Revolution –, but the Parliament voted against the proposal, citing financial difficulties. As an alternative, they proposed a national exhibition. On February 8, 1883, the Minister of Commerce tendered the construction of a large scale building installation for the Millennium Expo. The rights of both design and construction went to the architect Ignác Alpár. The main guidelines stated that the building should consist of three different parts which would represent the different styles of Hungarian architecture throughout the ages: a roman style, representing the Árpád-ages, a gothic one, and a renaissance-baroque part for the Habsburg era. Ignác Alpár created a picturesque installation of several buildings on the amorphous shaped Széchenyi Island in the City Gardens. It was inaugurated on May 1st, 1886, but as it was created exclusively for the expo, the building was designed to be only temporary. However, as the society stood up forcefully in support of the monument, it was reinforced with permanent, strong materials between 1902 and 1904. The main facade is the identical copy of Vajdahunyad Castle, thus being the reason behind the name of the complex. Other parts include Jáki chapel, the cloisters, the torture tower, the bridge gate, the auditorium, a lion shaped stone bridge, Segesvár (Sighisoara) Bastion Tower, Hunyadi-loggias, the Nyebojsza-tower, the dome facade, the Hunyadi court, a smaller version of Zápolya chapel, a copy of the Apostle Tower of Sighisoara Castle, the Hungarian Museum of Agriculture, the German facade, and the German and the French towers.

Városliget Skating Rink and the Rowing Lake

The Városliget Skating Rink was opened for the skating crowd on January 29th, 1870, inaugurated by crown prince Rudolph himself. Its construction was facilitated by the Pest Skating Association whose tireless lobbying activity resulted in the City Council's permission to create a seasonal skating rink on certain parts of the City Park Lake that could be used by any Budapest citizens free of charge. The first skating hall was a simple, two-room wooden building on the edge of the lake that tragically felt victim of the 1874 fire. Afterwards, the city authorities issued a new permit for the construction of a permanent building, which was accomplished by architect Ödön Lechner in a few years time. Between 2008 and 2012, the building underwent extensive renovations, thus regaining its old charm and beauty.

Budapest Zoo and Botanical Garden

The Budapest Zoo started to receive visitors as early as 1866, that qualifies it as the 26th oldest functioning zoo in the world. The main building was designed in art nouveau style, and its first inhabitant travelled here all the way from Vienna: Franz Joseph I and Sissi gave a giraffe as a present. During the reconstruction works of 1910, the Great Cliff was erected, that is the third of this type on the continent: only the Hamburg and Paris zoos have similar features. The Great Cliff also houses a water reservoir, that enables it to function as a water tower as well. Nowadays the Zoo is undergoing serious transformations. The thermal water of the Széchenyi Spa is being introduced as the main heating source, and an interactive exhibition space, called Magic Hill, is also being created inside the Great Cliff.

Széchenyi Spa

Budapest is worldwide renowned for being the city of spas and the impressive, yellow building of the Széchenyi Spa is one of the largest thermal spa complexes in Europe. The thermal water here was discovered by Vilmos Zsigmondy, a mining engineer, who made his first successful drilling in 1868. The first 'Artesian Spa' was inaugurated in 1881 in the City Gardens. The neo-baroque Széchenyi Thermal Spa was constructed in 1913, according to the designs of Győző

Czigler. It comprised a separate bathing area for males, females, and also a larger area of outdoor pools. The park side view of the building is one of the most dynamic structures created in the early 20th century. The interior of dome at the entrance gate is heavily decorated with monumental, art nouveau mosaics, which can provide enough sightseeing for a couple of hours. The northern wing of the building was inaugurated in 1927, enabling a quick access from the Állatkerti Way. Its neo-baroque interior houses different, more modernist structures. The entrance hall still preserves its original looks, and bears a unique atmosphere, significantly different from the other wings. Its 970 meter deep, 74,5 C hot thermal spring is one of the hottest ones in Europe. It is also used as a heating source for the Zoo.

Margaret Island

Situated in the middle of the Danube, embraced by Margaret and Árpád bridges Margaret Island is unquestionably the most beautiful park of Budapest. It got its present form in the 19th century, when, as a part of the Danube regulation procedure, the city decided to unify three neighbouring little isles: the Isles of Bath, Painter and Rabbit, to form a 2,5 kilometer long single entity. The isles were inhabited since the early Roman times, and they housed monasteries and royal hunting expeditions in the Middle Ages. Its name originates from Margaret, the daughter of King Bela IV, who, fulfilling her father's pledge, led a nun's life in the island's monastery at the end of the 13th century. Nowadays the Island houses several sporting grounds, hotels, and public parks, as well as a small, domestic zoo, a property of the Budapest Zoo, and Botanical Gardens.

Kopaszi Dam

The Kopaszi Dam is the first privately created and managed park of the Újbuda region. Situated just by the Lágymányos Bay, this 10 hectare large, modern park provides an excellent location for sports, picnics, or relaxation.

Budapest Arena, the 'Pebble'

In December 1999, the Hungarian Sports Arena, the country's only indoor facility with a capacity up to several thousand people, fell victim of an unfortunate fire. As the building was almost completely destroyed, the Hungarian population and the political elite almost unanimously supported the construction of a new venue. The French Bouygues construction giant was put in charge for the building of the new Arena. Affectionately called 'Pebble', the entire building was designed by Hungarian architects, in a close cooperation with Sports Concepts, an English-American design company. The construction works commenced on June 30th, 2011. The 'Pebble' swallowed 50 000 tons of concrete, 2 300 tons of steel, more than 11 000 000 screws and several kilometres of cables. It weighs more than Elizabeth Bridge and Liberty Bridge together. If we could weigh it somehow, the scale would go way over 200 000 tons. Its 25 000 square meter pedestrian area forms Hungary's largest granite covered territory. The Pebble was inaugurated on March 13th, 2003, with an impressive assembly of the greatest living Hungarian musicians. The gala ended with a virtuous performance of Beethoven's masterpiece, Symphony 9, which symbolized Hungary's approaching European Union membership. The Arena was named after the legendary Hungarian boxer, László Papp, on May 28th, 2004.

Puskás Ferenc Stadium

St. Stephen's Day, August 20

St. Stephen's Day is the oldest national holiday of Hungary, dating back to the 11th century, when King Ladislaus I changed its date from August 15 to August 20. This was the date when King Stephen I was canonized by Pope Gregory VII as Saint Stephen of Hungary in the Cathedral of Székesfehérvár. King Louis I acknowledged this date as a religious holiday, that was confirmed later by empress María Theresa. In 1771, St. Stephen's Holy Right Hand was exhibited in Vienna, and was later transferred to Budapest. After the Austro-Hungarian Compromise, August 20th regained its earlier importance, and was qualified as a bank holiday. After 1945, the holiday's national and religious content made it unacceptable for the new, communist leadership, and it was renamed first into the 'New Bread Fest', and later to the 'Day of the Constitution'. In 1991, the first democratically elected Parliament declared St. Stephen's day a national and religious holiday.

Night time panoramic view from
Hármashatár Hill

Batthyány Square
Market Hall

Main building
of Budapest University
of Economics and Technologies

Sun is setting behind the Matthias Church

We bid farewell from the lasts sparks of daylight behind Matthias Church,
but the city's bustle is eternal, its pulsation restless, as if it never needed to halt.

The ones produced this book ...

Attila P. Kovács
Author

He lives and breathes photography ever since elementary school. His first own project dates back to the age of 14, and ever since, his life has taken on new perspectives. After graduating from university, he was employed by the Mikroszámítógép Magazin (Microcomputer Journal) and the Új Alaplap, and he was a lecturer at the Faculty of Computer Science at ELTE University. Currently he teaches at the FotoArt Iskola, and also works for the Szép Élet Magazin.

Tibor Berta
Text writer

Theacher, guide, a lover of Budapest. After some time spent in the art world and book publishing he has been taking groups of tourists for boat trips on the Nile in Egypt. He worked for five years as editor, programme presenter of Civil Radio.

Ádám Lázár
Editor / proof-reader

His career in public journalism started in London as an editor of BBC's World News. He moved back to Hungary in 1996. He was Editor- in-Chief of Duna TV, and Hungarian Catholic Radio. Later, he was the Head of Press Department of the Ministry of Environment, and the Budapest Mayor's Office. He contributes articles and documentaries to Diplomatic Magazine, Explorer Magazine and National Geographic Magazine Hungary.

Sándor Király
Director of Production

He started his career as a graphic designer, swithed to work in a printer's office but he still reads, writes, and draws. He collects books no longer. He feels young at heart but he is sorry that he has not enough time to live through the life he already had. His task is to provide what is ordered from the print office and to achieve that he is helped by his outstanding work mates.

List of topics

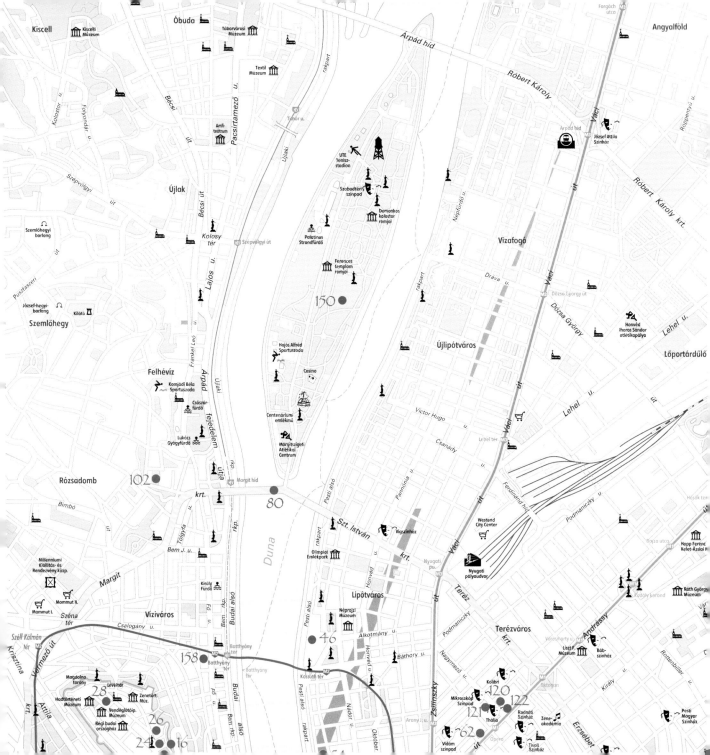

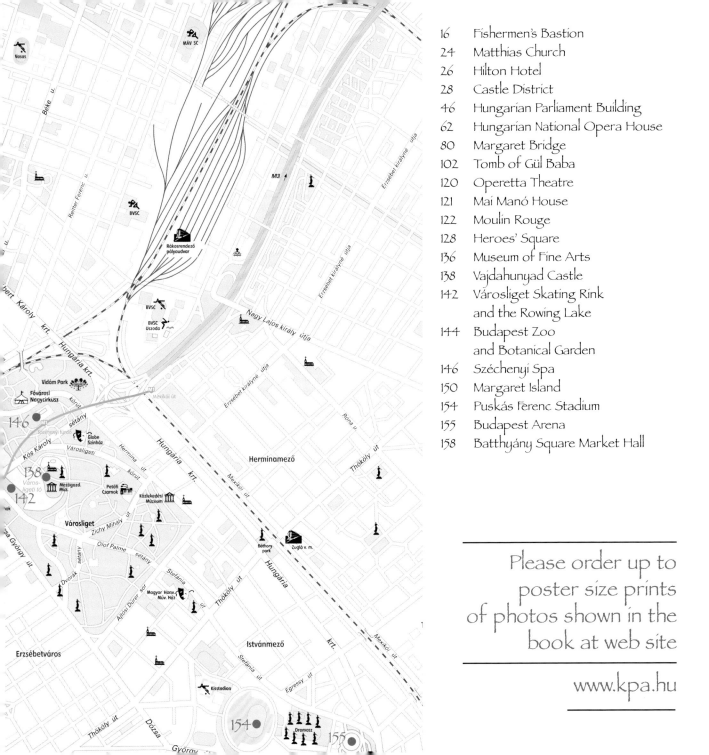

Please order up to
poster size prints
of photos shown in the
book at web site

www.kpa.hu

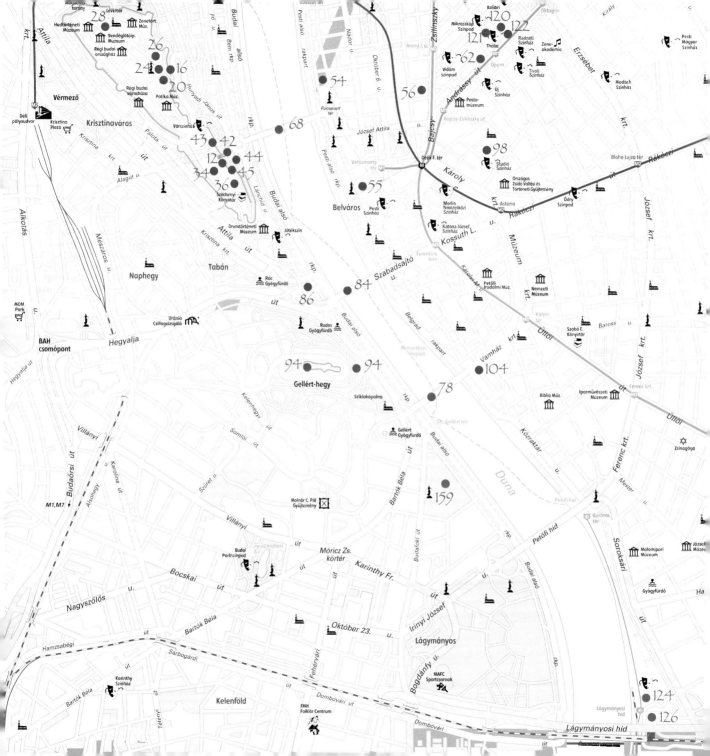

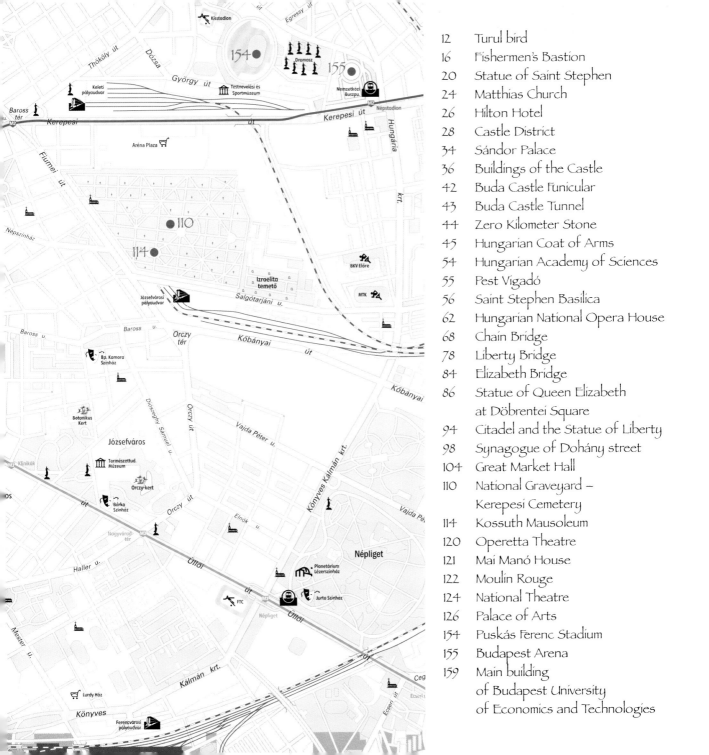